Nita Mehta's
CHOCOLATE
Cookbook

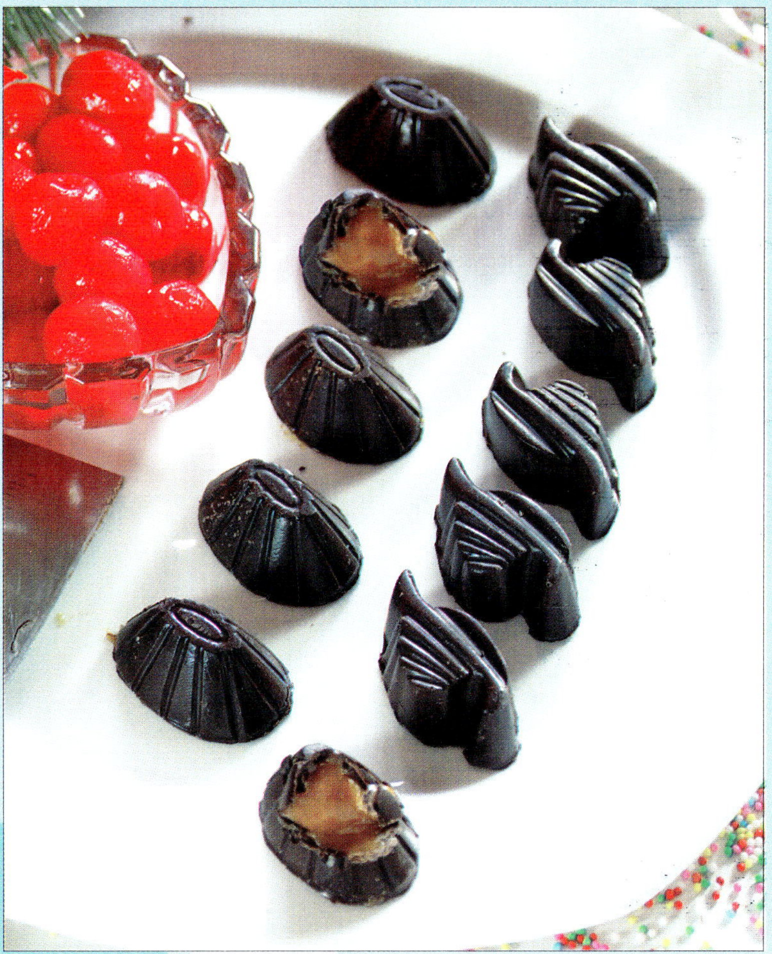

Nita Mehta's
CHOCOLATE
Cookbook

Nita Mehta

B.Sc. (Home Science)
M.Sc. (Food and Nutrition) Gold Medalist

© Copyright 2008 SNAB Publishers Pvt Ltd

WORLD RIGHTS RESERVED. The contents—all recipes, photographs and drawings are original and copyrighted. No portion of this book shall be reproduced, stored in a retrieval system or transmitted by any means, electronic, mechanical, photocopying, recording or otherwise, without the written permission of the publishers.

While every precaution is taken in the preparation of this book, the publisher and the author assume no responsibility for errors or omissions. Neither is any liability assumed for damages resulting from the use of information contained herein.

TRADEMARKS ACKNOWLEDGED. Trademarks used, if any, are acknowledged as trademarks of their respective owners. These are used as reference only and no trademark infringement is intended upon.

First Edition 2008

ISBN 978-81-7869-225-8

Food Styling and Photography:

Layout and laser typesetting :

N.I.T.A.
☎ 23252948
National Information Technology Academy
3A/3, Asaf Ali Road
New Delhi-110002

Contributing Writers :
Anurag Mehta
Subhash Mehta

Editorial & Proofreading :
Stephens Chako
Sangeeta

Published by :

Publishers Pvt. Ltd.
3A/3 Asaf Ali Road,
New Delhi - 110002
Tel: 23252948, 23250091
Telefax:91-11-23250091

Editorial and Marketing office:
E-159, Greater Kailash-II, N.Delhi-48
Fax:91-11-29225218, 29229558
Tel:91-11-29214011, 29218727, 29218574
E-Mail: nitamehta@email.com
snab@snabindia.com
Website:http://www.nitamehta.com
Website: http://www.snabindia.com

Distributed by :
THE VARIETY BOOK DEPOT
A.V.G. Bhavan, M 3 Con Circus,
New Delhi - 110 001
Tel : 23417175, 23412567; Fax : 23415335
Email: varietybookdepot@rediffmail.com

Printed by :
SANAT PRINTERS

Rs. 225/-

Introduction

Chocolate! The mere mention of anything associated with this mouthwatering confection can cause a dreamy look to come into the eyes of the chocoholic.

Different types of moulded chocolates have now become a favourite of many. There is nothing more satisfying than to offer a bunch of home made chocolates to your family and loved ones. Chocolate has long known to be an aphrodisiac and makes a beautiful gift for your beloved. And what could be better than a bowl of home made ones, specially to suit the taste of the person you are giving to. We have truffle chocolates, rich nutty rocks, minty ones, peanut caramel chocolates and more to choose from.

It is hard to resist the pleasure of a sumptuous piece of chocolate cake and no chocolate cookbook would be complete without a selection of cakes, gateaux and loaves - there are plenty to choose from in this chapter. A fine selection of tarts, cookies, donuts, eclairs will take care of the tea time treats. A chocolate dessert is always the grand finale of the meal. We offer the old favourites like the chocolate mousse along with many new creations. We have not left out on the chocolate decorations like flakes and scrolls or chocolate leaves to add that extra touch!

Nita Mehta

Contents

Introduction 5
Types of Chocolates 8
Storing Chocolate 9
Chopping Chocolate 9
Special Essences 9
Melting Chocolate in a Double Boiler 10
Melting Chocolate in a Microwave ... 10

11 Home Made Chocolates

Things needed for chocolate making 12
Must Read Tips 14
Fruit & Nut Bites 15
Truffle Balls 17
Basic Moulded Chocolates 18
Mint Chocolates 20
Rum Truffles 23
Variations of Truffles 24
Blue Berry Chocolates 25
Coconut Chocolates 26
Caramel Chocolates 28
Strawberry Chocolates 30
Mango Chocolates 32
Swirled Marble Chocolates 33
Crunchy Peanut Coins 34
Sticky Centre Chocolates 36
Boule D'amande 38
Spice Almond Chocolates 40
Rich Mocha Balls 41
Chocolate Wrapping 42
Chocolate Hearts 43
Chocolate Coated Fruits 44

45 Cakes Gateaux & Loaves

Quick Chocolate Cake 46
Chocolate -Vanilla Loaf 47
Chocolate Almond Cake.................. 48
Whole Wheat Honey Ginger Cake ... 50
Chocolate Orange Cake 51
Chocolate Truffle 52
Chocolate Tea Loaf 54
Toffee Cake 55
Swirled Ring Cake 57
Choco Orange Mousse Cake 58
Wild Strawberry Passion 60

62 Tea Time Treats

Chocolate Muffins 63
Choco Web Pie 64
Walnut Brownies 66
Chocolate Donuts............................ 68
Chocolate Swiss Rolls 71
Mocha Petit Fours 73
Chocolate Eclairs 74
Choco Truffle Tarts 77
Chocolate Chip Cookies 78
Pinwheel Biscuits 79
Double Choc Fudge Cake 80

83 Chocolate Desserts

Dark Chocolate Mousse 84
Striped Chocolate Cheese Cake 86
Chocolate Freezer Cake 88
Chocolate Marquis 90
Chocolate Decorations 92
Chocolate Sharts 94
Glossary 95
International Conversion Guide 96

Types of Chocolates

SEMISWEET / DARK CHOCOLATE:
52 to 62% cacao (cacao = cocoa solids + cocoa butter)

Semisweet chocolate is entry level for those who are new to bitter and darker, more pronounced chocolate flavour. This chocolate has a slightly sweet flavour and a dark brown colour. With its accessible flavour and creamy consistency, semisweet chocolate is a dream to work with. It melts easily, combines well with other flavours, and is fantastic for dipping.

BITTERSWEET :
63 to 72% cacao (cacao = cocoa solids + cocoa butter)

Darker and more pronounced in flavour than a semisweet, bittersweets are the favourites of many chefs. However, their higher cacao content can make them trickier to work with.

MILK CHOCOLATE:
36 to 46% cacao (cacao = cocoa solids + cocoa butter)

As the name suggests, it contains milk solids and has a creamy, mild and sweet flavour. It is light brown in colour and usually not recommended for cooking.

WHITE CHOCOLATE

Since it does not contain cacao solids, white chocolate is technically not a chocolate. Whether or not you're a fan of this bar of cocoa butter, sugar, vanilla, and milk, there are times when it is just right. White chocolate is very sensitive to heat, so be careful when melting it.

UNSWEETENED CHOCOLATE:
100% cacao

Unsweetened chocolate, as the name implies, is 100 percent cacao with no sugar added. One taste will tell you that it is not meant to be eaten alone. I like to use it in combination with semi or bittersweet to add depth of flavour. You can also improvise a bitter sweet by substituting about 20 percent unsweetened chocolate and 80 percent semisweet for the quantity of bittersweet specified in the recipe.

COCOA POWDER

Cocoa is the pure chocolate mass which is left when the cocoa butter has been removed from the chocolate liquor. It is then ground and sifted. Cocoa lends desserts and baked goods, a wonderful depth of flavour.

Storing Chocolate

Chocolate should be kept in its wrapper in a box and stored in a cool, dry dark place, away from direct sunlight or heat. If storing an opened bar, wrap in its paper and then in a sealed plastic bag. The best storage temperature is 62 to 70° F. I do not recommend refrigeration because the condensation that occurs can result in sugar bloom (or grains on the surface). If you live in a hot place without air conditioning, however, there may be no option. So, chocolate can be refrigerated in summer, but it is necessary to bring it to room temperature before chopping or grating. Chocolate melts in the low nineties - a pleasure when it's in your mouth and a potential disaster in a very hot kitchen.

The whitish colour that can rise to the top on chocolate is called fat bloom. It means the cocoa butter has separated and risen to the top due to heat. As unappealing as it looks, the final taste is not affected, because when the chocolate is melted, the cocoa butter will be redistributed throughout the chocolate.

Chopping Chocolate

To chop chocolate, the best tool is a long serrated knife and a heavy wooden board. Starting on a corner of a block or square of chocolate, cut ¼" thick slices along the diagonal, pressing both the hands on either side of the knife. The chocolate will naturally break into thin chips as you cut. Keep turning the chocolate square to work evenly off all the corners.

Special Essences

Moisture is a great enemy of chocolate. Even a drop of water can ruin the melted chocolate. Hence the choice of essence should be made carefully. Special oil bound essences are available for adding to the chocolate. The regular essences are water based and hence cannot be added to pure chocolate. However, these water based essences can be used in the centre fillings which are made with cream and icing sugar or in truffles where chocolate is mixed with cream to make the centre filling.

Melting Chocolate in a Double Boiler

Chocolate is very sensitive to heat and moisture. Once you learn the art of melting chocolate, working with it becomes very simple. Prevent any water or steam coming into contact with the melted chocolate. A small amount of liquid, even a wet spoon or steam may cause the chocolate to seize and stiffen, making it unusable.

1. The chocolate slab should be at room temperature at the time of melting. Cut the chocolate into thin pieces as given on page 9.

2. Put chocolate in a stainless steel bowl that can fit well over a sauce pan, without having space on the sides for the steam to escape. This makes a good double boiler. If steam goes into the melting chocolate, it may ruin the chocolate. Fill saucepan with 1" water and put it on fire to boil. When water boils, reduce heat to minimum.

3. Place the bowl of chocolate on the simmering water, making sure that the base of the bowl does not come into contact with water and the heat is very low. The water should not be boiling rapidly. Do not stir. Once the chocolate starts to melt, very gently stir with a rubber spatula or a spoon. When almost melted, switch off the fire.

4. Remove bowl from saucepan and place on a towel placed on the kitchen platform. This absorbs the moisture at the base of the bowl. Gently stir again for 2-3 minutes till fully melted, smooth and glossy.

Note: Do not melt chocolate over direct heat (unless melting with other ingredients - in this case keep the heat very low).

Melting Chocolate in a Microwave

This can be quite tricky at times. Melt very gradually, increasing the time only after checking the chocolate. Never melt the chocolate fully, once it softens it melts by itself on simply stirring it with a rubber spatula.

1. Cut the chocolate into small pieces. Place in a microwave-proof bowl.

2. Put the bowl in the microwave oven and melt. As a guide, melt 125 gm dark chocolate on high power for 1 minute and white or milk chocolate on medium power for 2-3 minutes.

3. Stir the chocolate with a spatula, let stand for a few minutes, then stir again if necessary. Return to the microwave for another 30 seconds if required.

Note: As microwave oven temperatures and settings vary, you should consult the manufacturer's instruction first.

Home Made Chocolates

Home Made Chocolates

Things needed for chocolate making

1. Heavy Wooden Chopping Board & a long Serrated Bread Knife:
A wooden chopping board is preferred to a plastic one for cutting the chocolate slab. See that the chopping board is absolutely clean. A long, serrated or saw edged knife makes cutting chocolate easier.

2. Chocolate Trays:
These are plastic trays with different designs. Choose a good quality tray. Wash and dry them thoroughly before use. Available at all kitchen stores.

3. Palette Knife:
This is long knife, either flexible or firm, with no sharp edges. It is rounded or square cut at the end. It is totally flat and is used to level chocolate in the tray for a neater finished look.

4. Rubber Spatula:
These are like flat spoons with a squarish rubber end. These are so flexible that they help take out all the melted chocolate from the bowl when it has to be transferred to the chocolate tray. It is also useful to stir the melted chocolate while it is being brought to room temperature after melting it. Stirring with the spatula not only cools down the chocolate but also tempers it, making it smooth and glossy.

5. Chocolate Scrapper:
Plastic as well as steel ones are available. A very useful tool in chocolate making as it cleans off all the chocolate from the surface. All the scraped chocolate can be melted again and reused.

6. Chocolate Fork:
A small fork with a wooden handle. Useful for draining off the excess chocolate when lifting truffle balls or cookies or fruit dipped in melted chocolate.

7. Chocolate Ring:
Useful while coating fruits or cookies with melted chocolate. This holds the fruit or cookie comfortably, draining off the excess chocolate at the same time.

8. Small Aluminium Pans & Non Stick Flat Pans:
Since the quantity of filling used in chocolates is quite less, having small pans is a good idea. Both aluminium and non stick ones work well.

9. Essences:
Special oil bound essences are available for mixing into the chocolate because the general essences are water based. Moisture or water added to melted chocolate can turn it into a lustreless hard mass. However, these water based essences can be added to mixtures prepared for the centres which have other ingredients like cream, icing sugar, butter etc.

Must Read Tips
To Make Perfect Chocolates

1. Usually the dark variety is better. Milk chocolates do not taste that good. Generally 100 gm chocolate when chipped is equal to about 1 cup.

2. Wipe chocolate trays with a muslin cloth. Even a drop of moisture in the tray will turn melted chocolate into a solid mass. Such chocolate cannot be used. When in a rush, using a hair dryer to dry the chocolate trays is a good idea.

3. Prepare a good double boiler for melting chocolate. See that no steam escapes from the sides of the bowl. Steam gives moisture to chocolate, turning it useless.

4. While melting chocolate, too much heat burns the chocolate. It loses it's lustre and shine. Keep the heat very low and put off the flame as soon as the chocolate softens. Sitting on the double boiler on hot water will melt the chocolate completely.

5. The prepared chocolates should preferably be set in the fridge and not in the freezer. The freezer has moisture in it.

6. When you fill the melted chocolate in the tray, quickly invert the mould and tap each mould just once to take out the excess. Do not tap too much, or you will not get a nice shell. Keep in the freezer for about 10 minutes to set.

7. To make centres with cream, use tetra packs of cream as they are stabilized and stay good for a long time. Fresh cream from the dairy should be avoided. Never heat the cream too much and never add chocolate to very hot cream. The fat separates on doing so. Remove the cream from heat and wait for a few seconds before you add the chocolate.

8. Let the filling come to room temperature before you put it in the chocolate shells. If you put hot filling you might end up having a chocolate with a hole.

9. When you put the centre in the shell for moulded chocolate, do not put too much of centre filling as it might come out of the chocolate covering. About ¼-½ tsp is enough in each shell. Leave enough space for the top layer of chocolate covering. Now keep in the fridge or freezer to set.

10. Before you put the final layer of melted chocolate, check that the filling is set.

Fruit & Nut Bites

Extremely simple to make!

Makes about 12

150 gms cooking chocolate - chopped
2-3 tbsp almonds - chopped, 2 tbsp walnuts - chopped, 3 tbsp raisins (*kishmish*)

1. Roast almonds and walnuts in a pan on very low heat, stirring continuously till fragrant. Add raisins and roast for another 2 minutes on low heat. Remove from pan as soon as the almonds start to change colour.

2. Melt the chocolate on a double boiler as given on page 10. Remove chocolate from heat. Stir till it comes to room temperature.

3. Stir in the nuts and raisins. Keep aside for a few minutes till it starts to become slightly thick. It should not be too runny, nor should you let it turn too thick.

4. With a spoon, drop rough heaps of the chocolate mixture onto a plate lined with aluminium foil.

5. Press nuts on top. Leave in the fridge to set before removing from the plate. Allow to set in the fridge for atleast 1-2 hours. Wrap in decorative paper Serve.

Truffle Balls

Soft, creamy truffle balls are covered with crisp chocolate. Serve in small paper cups for an elegant finale to a grand meal.

Makes 30-35

CENTRE
250 gms dark chocolate - chipped or cut into small pieces
100 gm (½ cup) cream, (any tetra pack cream)
1½ - 2 tbsp of rum or 1 tsp rum essence, optional, 1 tbsp icing sugar to coat

COVERING
250 gm dark chocolate - chipped
50 gm white chocolate - chipped (½ cup), for making lines

1. Warm cream in a heavy bottomed saucepan, on low heat. Do not boil.

2. Add chipped chocolate. Cook on very low heat stirring continuously for about 5 minutes, till the sauce thickens and starts leaving the sides. Remove from fire. Wait for a minute. Add rum. Mix well. Transfer to a small bowl. When you remove the mixture from fire it is thin but it firms up on keeping.

3. Put truffle mixture in the freezer for atleast ½-1 hour or till firm enough to make round balls. Make balls.

4. Roll in icing sugar to coat. Place on a plate lined with aluminium foil. Keep in the fridge.

5. Once the balls are set, melt the chocolate for covering as given on page 10. Remove the melted chocolate from the hot water and stir with a rubber spatula for 2 minutes till it becomes glossy & cools down to room temperature.

6. Add 3-4 balls to the melted chocolate. Stir with a fork to coat chocolate. Remove balls from the melted chocolate. Shake off the excess. Place chocolate coated balls on the foil.

7. Make a tight paper bag and secure with scotch tape. Melt white chocolate in the microwave for 30 seconds till soft. Mix well to make a smooth paste. Put melted chocolate in a paper bag. Pipe lines on the chocolate. Refrigerate for 3-4 hours.

Basic Moulded Chocolates

Chocolates can be made into different shapes using a plastic chocolate tray with different shaped moulds. A variety of fillings can be used to fill chocolates. The recipe of various fillings for the centre of chocolates follow later. Here we give you the basic way for making all chocolates with centre fillings. The variety of centre fillings follow later.

Makes 1 chocolate tray

150 gm dark chocolate - cut into small pieces

1. Prepare the centre filling. Keep filling aside. Melt covering chocolate in a double boiler as given on page 10. Remove from hot water on a kitchen towel spread on the kitchen platform to absorb any moisture at the bottom of the bowl. Keep stirring with a rubber spatula for 2-3 minutes to temper the chocolate and bring it to room temperature. The chocolate will turn very smooth and glossy. Do not fill hot chocolate into the tray.

2. Spoon melted chocolate in chocolate tray to fill the moulds fully. Tap on the kitchen surface 1-2 times.

3. Invert the tray, holding the tray over the cleaned kitchen platform for the extra chocolate to come out and the chocolate left just coats the mould. If you like, tap 1-2 times with a palette knife to remove the extra chocolate to make thin shells.

4. Invert to get the right side up. Level chocolate with a palette knife, dropping the excess chocolate on the kitchen slab. Keep tray in the freezer for 10 minutes.

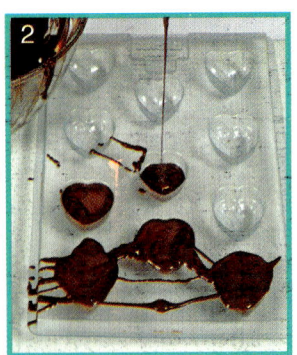

5. Scrape the chocolate on the kitchen platform and put it in the bowl of chocolate. Keep the chocolate bowl back on hot water in the double boiler.

6. Take out the set chocolate tray. Spoon ¼ - ½ tsp of filling mixture in each shell, pushing the filling into the shell with the help of a table knife, if need be. Keep in the fridge to set for 10-15 minutes. Do not fill too much, keep ¼ of the shell empty.

7. When the filling feels slightly set when touched with a finger, spoon melted chocolate over the filling to cover the filling completely.

8. Spoon chocolate generously it till it comes out a little from the sides. This over filling of the covering chocolate seals the filling nicely. Shake the tray lightly to level. Do not tap the tray.

9. Scrape off the excess chocolate gently with a palette knife. Run the knife once forwards and then backwards. Keep tray in the fridge to set for at least 2 hours.

10. Invert the tray and tap lightly to unmould the chocolates.
11. Neaten the edges of the chocolate using a knife. Store covered and refrigerated.
12. Scrape the chocolate on the kitchen platform with a chocolate scraper. This chocolate can be melted again and reused.

Mint Chocolates

A green mint filling with a soft texture. It is essential to use icing sugar for this filling. Do not choose very deep moulds for this chocolate as the filling is quite sweet and you need to fill just a small quantity of it.

Makes 10 - 12 (one tray)

CENTRE
4 tbsp sifted icing sugar, 2 tbsp cream
10 polo mint sweets - crushed to a powder and sifted, a drop of green colour, optional

COVERING CHOCOLATE
150 gm dark cooking chocolate - cut into small pieces

1. To prepare the mint centre, mix cream, crushed mint sweet and icing sugar in a small heavy bottomed pan. Cook on low heat stirring continuously for 1 minute. Do not cook longer. (It should have a thick pouring consistency when you remove it from fire. When it cools, it turns to a sticky paste). Add just enough colour to get a pale green filling. If you like, do not add colour and leave the filling white. Keep aside till the chocolate shells are ready.

2. Melt covering chocolate in a double boiler. Remove from hot water on a kitchen towel spread on the kitchen platform to absorb any moisture at the bottom of the bowl. Keep stirring with a rubber spatula for 2-3 minutes to temper the chocolate and bring it to room temperature. Do not fill hot chocolate into the tray.

3. Spoon melted chocolate in chocolate tray to fill the moulds nicely. Tap 1-2 times.

4. Invert the tray and holding the tray over the cleaned kitchen platform, tap 1-2 times with a palette knife to remove the extra chocolate and make shells.

5. Invert to get the right side up. Scrape off the excess chocolate with a palette knife. Keep tray in the freezer for 10 minutes. Keep the remaining chocolate on hot water in the double boiler.

6. Take out the set chocolate tray. Spoon ¼ - ½ tsp of filling in each shell, pushing the filling into the shell with the help of a table knife. Keep in the fridge to set.

7. When the filling is slightly set, spoon melted chocolate to cover the top. Spoon chocolate generously till it comes out a little from the sides. This seals the filling.

8. Scrape off the excess chocolate gently with a palette knife and put the scraped chocolate back in the chocolate bowl in the double boiler on hot water. Keep the tray in the fridge to set for at least 2 hours. Invert the tray and tap lightly to unmould the chocolates. Store covered and refrigerated.

Rum Truffles

For chocolates with special centres, it is a good idea to make the centres first and then melt the covering chocolate. It is not always safe to reheat the melted chocolate if it starts to set again while the centre filling is being made. Also, the centre becomes cold and firms up before putting in the chocolate shells if made before melting the chocolate.

Makes one tray (11-12 pieces)

RUM CENTRE
40 gms chocolate - cut into small pieces (5 tbsp chipped)
3 tbsp thick cream, 1 tsp rum

COVERING CHOCOLATE
150 gm dark cooking chocolate - cut into small pieces

1. To prepare the centre, warm the cream in a small nonstick pan or a heavy bottomed small kadhai. Do not bring to a boil. Add chocolate to it. Remove from fire. Mix well till smooth with a wooden spoon . Let the chocolate cool completely. Add rum to it. Keep truffle filling aside till the chocolate shells are set.

2. Melt covering chocolate in a double boiler. Remove from hot water on a kitchen towel spread on the kitchen platform to absorb any moisture at the bottom of the bowl. Keep stirring with a rubber spatula for 2-3 minutes to temper the chocolate and bring it to room temperature. Do not fill hot chocolate into the tray.

3. Spoon melted chocolate in chocolate tray to fill the moulds nicely. Tap 1-2 times.

4. Invert the tray and holding the tray over the cleaned kitchen platform, tap 1-2 times with a palette knife to remove the extra chocolate and make shells.

5. Invert to get the right side up. Scrape off the excess chocolate with a palette knife. Keep tray in the freezer for 10 minutes. Keep the remaining chocolate on hot water in the double boiler.

6. Take out the set chocolate tray. Spoon ¼ - ½ tsp of filling in each shell, pushing the filling into the shell with the help of a table knife. Keep in the fridge to set.

7. When the filling is slightly set, spoon melted chocolate to cover the top. Spoon chocolate generously it till it comes out a little from the sides. This seals the filling.

8. Scrape off the excess chocolate gently with a palette knife and put the scraped chocolate back in the chocolate bowl in the double boiler on hot water. Keep the tray in the fridge to set for at least 2 hours. Invert the tray and tap lightly to unmould the chocolates. Store covered and refrigerated.

Variations of Truffles

Orange Truffle

Add 3-4 drops of orange essence instead of rum at step 1. Follow the rest of the recipe given on page 23.

Coffee Truffle

Add ½ tsp coffee instead of rum at step 1. Mix coffee with a tsp of warm water before adding. Follow the rest of the recipe given on page 23.

Almond Truffle

(White Chocolate Truffle)

Warm 3 tbsp thick cream, remove from fire and add 40 gms chipped white chocolate (5 tbsp). Mix well and cool slightly. Add 2-3 drops of sweet almond essence. Keep filling aside till the shells are ready. Follow the rest of the recipe given on page 23.

Blue Berry Chocolates

A moulded chocolate with a soft jam filling. You can use the jam of your choice.

Makes one tray (11-12 pieces)

JAM CENTRE
3 tbsp blue berry jam, 1 tbsp fresh cream

COVERING CHOCOLATE
150 gm dark cooking chocolate - cut into small pieces

1. To prepare the centre, heat the jam in a nonstick pan. Add cream to it and mix well till smooth with a plastic or wooden spoon. Remove from fire. Keep aside.

2. Melt covering chocolate in a double boiler. Remove from hot water on a kitchen towel spread on the kitchen platform to absorb any moisture at the bottom of the bowl. Keep stirring with a rubber spatula for 2-3 minutes to temper the chocolate and bring it to room temperature. Do not fill hot chocolate into the tray.

3. Spoon melted chocolate in chocolate tray to fill the moulds nicely. Tap 1-2 times.

4. Invert the tray and holding the tray over the cleaned kitchen platform, tap 1-2 times with a palette knife to remove the extra chocolate and make shells.

5. Invert to get the right side up. Scrape off the excess chocolate with a palette knife. Keep tray in the freezer for 10 minutes.

6. Keep the remaining chocolate on hot water in the double boiler.

7. Take out the set chocolate tray. Spoon $\frac{1}{4}$ - $\frac{1}{2}$ tsp of filling mixture in each shell, pushing the filling into the shell with the help of a table knife. Keep in the fridge to set. (Do not fill too much)

8. When the filling is slightly set, spoon melted chocolate to cover the top. Spoon chocolate generously it till it comes out a little from the sides. This seals the filling.

9. Scrape off the excess chocolate gently with a palette knife and put the scraped chocolate back in the chocolate bowl in the double boiler on hot water. Keep the tray in the fridge to set for at least 2 hours. Invert the tray and tap lightly to unmould the chocolates. Store covered and refrigerated.

Coconut Chocolates

Coconut chocolates acquire an off flavour if kept for too many days. The coconut filling can also be rolled into balls and dipped in melted chocolate.

Makes one tray (11-12 pieces)

3 tbsp icing sugar, 4 tbsp desiccated coconut
2 tbsp milk powder, 2 tbsp cream
COVERING CHOCOLATE
150 gm dark cooking chocolate - cut into small pieces

1. To prepare the centre, mix cream, coconut, milk powder & icing sugar in a small heavy bottomed pan or kadhai. Cook on low heat stirring continuously for a minute to mix well. Do not cook longer. It should not turn hard and dry. Keep aside in the fridge till the chocolate shells are set.

2. Melt covering chocolate in a double boiler. Remove from hot water on a kitchen towel spread on the kitchen platform to absorb any moisture at the bottom of the bowl. Keep stirring with a rubber spatula for 2-3 minutes to temper the chocolate and bring it to room temperature. Do not fill hot chocolate into the tray.

3. Spoon melted chocolate in chocolate tray to fill the moulds nicely. Tap 1-2 times.

4. Invert the tray and holding the tray over the cleaned kitchen platform, tap 1-2 times with a palette knife to remove the extra chocolate and make shells.

5. Invert to get the right side up. Scrape off the excess chocolate with a palette knife. Keep tray in the freezer for 10 minutes. Keep the remaining chocolate on hot water in the double boiler.

6. Take out the set chocolate tray. Spoon ¼ - ½ tsp of filling mixture in each shell, pushing the filling into the shell with the help of a table knife. Keep in the fridge to set. (Do not fill too much.)

7. When the filling is slightly set, spoon melted chocolate to cover the top. Spoon chocolate generously it till it comes out a little from the sides. This seals the filling.

8. Scrape off the excess chocolate gently with a palette knife and put the scraped chocolate back in the chocolate bowl in the double boiler on hot water. Keep the tray in the fridge to set for at least 2 hours. Invert the tray and tap lightly to unmould the chocolates. Store covered and refrigerated.

Note: Desiccated coconut should be stored in the fridge as the oil in it turns rancid. Even milk powder needs to be refrigerated.

Caramel Chocolates

Makes one tray (11 pieces)

CENTRE
4 tbsp grain sugar
4 tbsp thin cream (to be at room temp), 1 tbsp water at room temp.

COVERING CHOCOLATE
150 gm dark cooking chocolate - cut into small pieces

1. To prepare the centre, measure cream and keep ready in a small bowl. Spread the sugar in a small flat aluminium pan. Keep on medium heat, without touching or stirring for about 2 minutes. When the sides turn light golden, lift the pan off the fire and rotate the pan gently to evenly brown the sugar. Return to fire on low heat for 1-2 minutes. When sugar melts properly and it turns a rich golden, remove from fire. Add cream and mix well with a spoon till smooth. Add 1 tbsp water. Mix well with a spoon. Cook caramel for 5-7 seconds to get a smooth consistency. Remove from fire. Remove caramel from pan to a bowl immediately to avoid over cooking it on the hot pan. Keep aside.

2. Melt covering chocolate in a double boiler. Remove from hot water on a kitchen towel spread on the kitchen platform to absorb any moisture at the bottom of the bowl. Keep stirring with a rubber spatula for 2-3 minutes to temper the chocolate and bring it to room temperature. Do not fill hot chocolate into the tray.

3. Spoon melted chocolate in chocolate tray to fill the moulds nicely. Tap 1-2 times.

4. Invert the tray and holding the tray over the cleaned kitchen platform, tap 1-2 times with a palette knife to remove the extra chocolate and make shells.

5. Invert to get the right side up. Scrape off the excess chocolate with a palette knife. Keep tray in the freezer for 10 minutes. Keep the remaining chocolate on hot water in the double boiler.

6. Take out the set chocolate tray. Spoon ¼ - ½ tsp of filling in each shell, pushing the filling into the shell with the help of a table knife. Keep in the fridge to set.

7. When the filling is slightly set, spoon melted chocolate to cover the top. Spoon chocolate generously it till it comes out a little from the sides. This seals the filling.

8. Scrape off the excess chocolate gently with a palette knife and put the scraped chocolate back in the chocolate bowl in the double boiler on hot water. Keep the tray in the fridge to set for at least 2 hours. Invert the tray and tap lightly to unmould the chocolates. Store covered and refrigerated.

Strawberry Chocolates

A pink strawberry filling with a soft texture. Keep a thin layer of filling as it is a little sweet.

Makes one tray (11-12 pieces)

CENTRE
6 tbsp sifted icing sugar, 4 tbsp thick cream, 1 tsp cornflour
½ tsp strawberry essence, a drop of pink or red colour

COVERING CHOCOLATE
150 gms dark cooking chocolate - cut into small pieces

1. To prepare the centre, mix cream, icing sugar and cornflour in a small heavy bottomed pan or kadhai. Cook on low heat stirring continuously for 3-4 minutes with the spatula till it becomes slightly thick and the raw taste of cornflour disappears. Add essence and colour. Keep aside till the chocolate shells are set.

2. Melt covering chocolate in a double boiler. Remove from hot water on a kitchen towel spread on the kitchen platform to absorb any moisture at the bottom of the bowl. Keep stirring with a rubber spatula for 2-3 minutes to temper the chocolate and bring it to room temperature. Do not fill hot chocolate into the tray.

3. Spoon melted chocolate in chocolate tray to fill the moulds nicely. Tap 1-2 times.

4. Invert the tray and holding the tray over the cleaned kitchen platform, tap 1-2 times with a palette knife to remove the extra chocolate and make shells.

5. Invert to get the right side up. Scrape off the excess chocolate with a palette knife. Keep tray in the freezer for 10 minutes.

6. Keep the remaining chocolate on hot water in the double boiler.

7. Take out the set chocolate tray. Spoon ¼ - ½ tsp of filling mixture in each shell, pushing the filling into the shell with the help of a table knife. Keep in the fridge to set. (Do not fill too much.)

8. When the filling is slightly set, spoon melted chocolate to cover the top. Spoon chocolate generously it till it comes out a little from the sides. This seals the filling.

9. Scrape off the excess chocolate gently with a palette knife and put the scraped chocolate back in the chocolate bowl in the double boiler on hot water. Keep the tray in the fridge to set for at least 2 hours. Invert the tray and tap lightly to unmould the chocolates. Store covered and refrigerated.

Mango Chocolates

Children will love this great combination of fruity chocolate. Chocolate can also be made in specially designed moulds for kids. Use a combination of white and dark chocolate.

Makes one tray (11-12 pieces)

200 gms white cooking chocolate - cut into small pieces
½ tsp mango essence (any other essence of your choice can be used)
a few drops yellow or orange colour

1. Melt white chocolate in a double boiler till it starts to melt on the edges. Remove from hot water and stir till it turns smooth.
2. Add essence and colour.
3. Spoon the mango chocolate in each shell to fill. Gently tap. Scrape off the excess chocolate gently with a palette knife. Keep the tray in the fridge to set for at least 3- 4 hours.
4. Invert mould. Tap lightly to unmould the chocolates. Store covered and refrigerated.

Swirled Marble Chocolates

Children as well as adults will love this great combination of white and dark chocolate.

Makes one tray (11-12 pieces)

125 gms white cooking chocolate - cut into small pieces
75 gms dark cooking chocolate - cut into small pieces

1. Melt dark chocolate on hot water in the double boiler. Remove from hot water. Stir till the chocolate becomes smooth. Keep aside.

2. Melt the white chocolate also on hot water in the double boiler. Remove from hot water. Stir till the chocolate becomes smooth.

3. Gently pour the melted dark chocolate just in the centre of the melted white chocolate in the bowl. Do not mix.

4. With a tablespoon, gently spoon out the chocolate from the side of the bowl to get both white and dark chocolate in the spoon. Pour in the tray in the moulds. Keep the tray in the fridge to set for at least 2 hours.

Crunchy Peanut Coins

Caramelized peanut coins dipped in melted chocolate.

Makes 10

CENTRE
¼ cup roasted peanuts - roughly crushed

4 tbsp sugar

2 tbsp butter (softened)

2 tbsp water

COVERING CHOCOLATE
100 gm cooking chocolate - cut into small pieces

1. To prepare the centre, measure butter and keep ready in a small bowl. Spread the sugar in a small flat aluminium pan. Keep on medium heat for about 2 minutes, without touching or stirring. When the sides turn light golden, lift the pan off the fire and rotate the pan gently to evenly brown the sugar. Return to fire on low heat for 1-2 minutes till sugar melts properly and turns a rich golden colour. Remove from fire.

2. Add butter and mix well with a spoon till smooth. Add 2 tbsp water. Mix well with a spoon. Cook caramel on low heat for a minute to get a smooth consistency.

3. Add roasted peanuts to it and stir well. Remove praline mix from fire. Mix very well continuously with a spoon for 1-2 minutes till the caramel starts to become thick and coat the peanuts. Transfer to the kitchen platform. Keep mixing it with a spoon for 1-2 minutes till it cools enough to be formed into balls. Do not cool too much, otherwise it hardens and becomes difficult to roll them into balls.

4. Make 10 tiny balls with the praline mix. Flatten each slightly to a coin shape.

5. Melt 100 gms of covering chocolate on a double boiler. Put praline coins into it, one at a time & roll nicely with a fork to coat each ball.

6. Lift the balls with the help of a fork and place them on a plate lined with aluminium foil. Keep in the fridge to set. You can give them a second dip in the melted chocolate if you like a thicker coating of chocolate.

Sticky Centre Chocolates

Do not choose a very deep mould for this chocolate, only a small amount is good in the chocolate as it is a sticky filling.

Makes 20-22

CENTRE
3 tbsp liquid glucose
3 tbsp sugar syrup of one string consistency, see in the method
½ -1 tsp orange or strawberry essence or any flavour of your choice
a pinch of colour

COVERING CHOCOLATE
250 gm dark cooking chocolate - cut into small pieces

1. To prepare the syrup, boil ¼ cup sugar and ¼ cup water. Keep on medium flame for about 5 minutes till a one string consistency is ready. The syrup feels sticky when pulled between the thumb and the forefinger. Keep aside.

2. Mix 3 tbsp liquid glucose with 2 tbsp of the above syrup. Add essence and colour. Keep in the fridge to become slightly thick as it cools down.

3. Melt covering chocolate in a double boiler. Remove from hot water and stir till it comes to room temperature. Do not fill hot chocolate into the tray. Spoon melted chocolate in the chocolate tray to fill the moulds nicely. Tap once on the surface.

4. Invert the tray and tap the backside of each line of the tray 1-2 times with a palette knife to remove the extra chocolate and make shells. Invert to get the right side up. Scrape off the excess chocolate on the tray around the moulds with a palette knife. Keep tray in the freezer for 10 minutes. Scrape chocolate from the kitchen surface and put it in the chocolate bowl. Keep the chocolate bowl on hot water in the double boiler.

5. Take out the set chocolate tray. Spoon ¼ - ½ tsp of filling in each shell, pushing the filling into the shell with the help of a table knife. Keep in the fridge to set.

6. When the filling is slightly set, spoon melted chocolate to cover the top. Spoon chocolate generously it till it comes out a little from the sides. This seals the filling.

7. Scrape off the excess chocolate gently with a palette knife and put the scraped chocolate back in the chocolate bowl in the double boiler on hot water. Keep the tray in the fridge to set for at least 2 hours. Invert the tray and tap lightly to unmould the chocolates. Store covered and refrigerated.

Boule D'amande

These elegant milk chocolate spheres have it all - a creamy milk chocolate centre, a crisp dark chocolate shell, and a crunchy coating of toasted nuts. Make sure to scoop out small enough centres since the little balls keep growing as they take on their coatings.

Makes 20-25 pieces

250 gms milk chocolate - chipped or cut into small pieces
100 gm heavy cream, any tetra pack cream will do

COVERING
250 gm dark chocolate - cut into small pieces
1 cup whole almonds - toasted in a pan for 3-4 minutes till fragrant and then chopped

1. Place cream in a heavy bottom saucepan, on low heat.
2. Heat till cream is warm but do not boil as this will cause curdling.
3. Remove from heat and add chipped milk chocolate. Stir well with a rubber spatula till all the chocolate melts. (If the chocolate does not melt fully you can again reheat for a short while on low heat).
4. Pour into a bowl. Cover with a wrap and keep in the fridge for 2-3 hours until firm enough to scoop out into balls.
5. Make round balls, about ¾" diameter.
6. Spread almonds on a tray or a cookie sheet.
7. For the outer covering, cut 250 gm cooking chocolate into small pieces.
8. Take a pan ¼ filled with water and heat till boiling. Lower the heat to the minimum.
9. Take another slightly bigger stainless steel or any heat proof bowl. See that it is dry and absolutely clean. Put the chocolate bits in it and place the bowl on the pan of hot water in such a way that the bottom of the bowl does not touch the water. (This works as a double boiler). Do not stir and wait for 3 minutes till chocolate starts to melt.
10. The chocolate will melt slowly. When a little melted, shut off the fire. Do not wait for it to get fully melted. With a rubber spatula, stir after removing from water till fully melted. If need be return the bowl on the pan of hot water but do not put on the fire. The little heat will melt those lumps away. Stir with the spatula to dissolve lumps.
11. Immediately dip balls in this melted chocolate to coat evenly. Pick up with a fork and drop off the excess chocolate.
12. Then immediately drop each chocolate in the nuts. Wait for 5-10 seconds, then roll to completely cover. Let set for 2-3 minutes, transfer to an aluminium foil lined tray and let it set. After setting in fridge for 10-12 hours wrap in coloured cellophane or silver or gold paper. Always keep in the refrigerator.

Spice Almond Chocolates

These are spiced chocolate balls without an outer chocolate coating. These make a good digestive end with coffee to a formal meal. Serve them in small paper cups with coffee after dinner. Do not wrap them in paper.

Makes 14-15

80 gms chocolate - cut into tiny pieces (¾ cup)

3 tbsp thick cream

SPICES (CRUSH TOGETHER TO A POWDER)
seeds of 1 green cardamom (*chhoti illaichi*), 1 clove (*laung*)
½" stick cinnamon (*dalchini*), a pinch of nutmeg powder (*jaiphal*)

TO COAT
¼ cup almonds - chopped finely and roasted

1. Heat cream in a heavy bottom sauce pan on low heat. Add chocolate to it. Remove from fire. Mix well with a rubber spatula. Add all spices and mix well.

2. Keep in the fridge for 1 hour or in the freezer for 15-20 minutes to set well enough to form balls. Make small marble sized balls.

3. Roll them in the roasted almonds. Put in the fridge for 2-3 hours till they set well.

Rich Mocha Balls

The word mocha suggests a combination of chocolate and coffee.

Makes 10

30 gm unsalted butter - melted (3 tbsp approx.)
50 gm dark chocolate - cut into small pieces (½ cup)
1½ tsp coffee mixed with 1 tsp water, 1 tsp rum or chocolate liquor
½ cup chocolate cake crumbs (crush 3 slices of any cake)

TO COAT
3 tbsp desiccated coconut

1. Mix coffee with water and keep aside.
2. Melt butter on low heat. Remove from fire. Add chocolate to it. Mix well till smooth.
3. Add coffee paste & rum to the chocolate mixture.
4. Mix cake crumbs & keep it in the fridge till set for about 1 hour.
5. Make small lemon sized balls and gently roll them in desiccated coconut spread in a plate. Keep chocolate balls in the fridge & serve them in small paper cups.

Chocolate Wrapping

Beautiful paper wrappings with dainty ribbons make chocolates look very attractive. Choose the colour of the paper according to the flavour, like green paper for a mint chocolate, silver for almond truffles, gold for caramel, pink for strawberry and so on. If you are making 3-4 flavours, always wrap a particular flavour in the same coloured wrapper. It becomes easier to choose your kind of chocolate. Follow these steps for a simple, yet elegant packing...

1. Unmould the chocolates and carefully trim the edges of the chocolate with a sharp pair of scissors as shown on page 19, step 11. Do not try to break them. Place in a plate and cover with a cling wrap. Return chocolates to the fridge for 2-3 hours so that they turn cold again before they are packed. (The chocolate trimmings can be melted with more chocolate and reused.)

2. Place the chocolate on a square piece of wrapper and fold the four sides as you do for packing a gift. Once covered with the paper, press the top part gently to get impressions of the chocolate on the paper.

3. Cut a square piece of a cellophane sheet, about 4-5", much bigger than the chocolate. Place the wrapped chocolate on it. Lift the sides of the cellophane and collect at the top, like a pouch (*potli*).

4. Tie a very thin satin ribbon to secure the frill on the top. Cut the edges of the ribbon diagonally to avoid fraying of the ribbon. Randomly cut off the extra cellophane on the top with a pair of scissors. Refrigerate.

Chocolate Hearts

A quick bite for your child and his/her friends.

Makes 15

1 pack of little hearts (biscuits)
100 gm chocolate - cut into small pieces
a plate lined with aluminium foil
1 tsp sesame seeds - roasted, optional

1. Melt the chocolate as given on page 10, in a double boiler.

2. Dip the heart biscuits in the melted chocolate, one at a time. Remove the biscuit with a fork so that the extra chocolate falls off.

3. Place chocolate coated biscuits on a plate lined with aluminium foil. Sprinkle a pinch of roasted sesame seeds. Keep in the fridge to set for about an hour.

Chocolate Coated Fruits

Strawberries coated with melted white or dark chocolate and chilled in the fridge to set. Even yellow raspberries and oranges work well. Use them to decorate cakes or desserts or enjoy them plain with a dollop of ice cream or just with coffee. They should be used within a day or two.

Serves 8

50 gm (¼ cup) cream

100 gm cooking chocolate, white or dark - cut into small pieces

TO COAT

strawberries or raspberries or goose berries

an orange separated into segments or roasted almonds

1. Warm cream on very low heat in a heavy bottom pan, but do not boil.
2. Add white or dark chocolate pieces and stir on low heat till chocolate starts to melt. Remove from fire. Stir with a rubber spatula till smooth. Let it cool to room temperature.
3. Hold the fruit with the fork from the leaves and dip ½ of the fruit in the prepared chocolate icing, leaving the top of the fruit and leaves uncoated. Place on the greased aluminium foil or grease proof paper. Keep in the fridge for the chocolate to set. Similarly dip the end of a whole roasted almond to make chocolate nuts.

Strawberries dipped in white chocolate

Raspberries dipped in dark chocolate

Cakes Gateaux & Loaves

Quick Chocolate Cake

Serves 8

4 large eggs
1¼ cups powdered sugar
1 tsp vanilla essence
¾ cup oil
½ cup cocoa powder
1 cup flour (*maida*)
¾ tsp baking powder
a pinch soda-bi-carb (*mitha soda*)

1. Beat eggs and powdered sugar in a bowl with an electric egg beater till more than double in volume and very frothy. Add essence.
2. To make beating quicker, you can place the bowl of eggs and sugar over a small saucepan of boiling water (fill about 1" water in the sauce pan). The bottom of the bowl should not touch the water.
3. Add oil gradually to the frothy eggs and keep beating slowly.
4. Sift flour, baking powder, cocoa and soda-bi-carb. Sprinkle ½ of the maida mixture on the egg mixture. Using a wooden spoon, with an upward and downward motion, fold in flour gently. Sprinkle the remaining flour also. Do not over mix. Fold in all the flour gently.
5. Transfer to a greased round tin of 8" diameter & bake at 180°C/350°F for 30-35 minutes.
6. Test cake by inserting a clean knife in centre of the cake. If it comes out clean, cake is ready. Remove from the oven. Remove the cake from the tin after 5 minutes.

Chocolate -Vanilla Loaf

A two coloured eggless cake. Very simple to prepare, yet good to look at!

Serves 6-8

½ tin condensed milk (milk maid), 2 tbsp powdered sugar
1 tsp vanilla essence, 1¼ cups (125 gm) flour (*maida*)
¾ tsp soda-bicarb, ¾ tsp baking powder, ½ cup oil
100 ml (½ cup) milk, 1 tbsp cocoa powder

1. Sieve flour, baking powder and soda together. Keep aside.
2. Mix condensed milk, sugar & essence. Add oil in a stream and keep beating till well blended.
3. Add half of the flour. Add half of the milk. Mix well. Add the remaining milk and flour. Beat well for 3-4 minutes till the mixture is light and fluffy.
4. Divide into 2 parts. To one part add cocoa & mix well. Grease a 9" long loaf tin. Put the plain mixture in the cake tin. On top of it spread the chocolate mixture. Swirl a spoon lightly in the mixture to get the marble effect.

5. Smoothen the top. Bake in a preheated oven at 150°C/300°F for 40 min. Insert a clean knife in the centre of the cake. If it comes out clean, switch off the oven. Remove from oven after 5 minutes.

47

Chocolate Almond Cake

Makes about 1¼ kg, serves 16, a big baking tin of 11-12" diameter is required, so make half the quantity if you have a small cake tin for baking.

Makes 16

1 tin (400 gm) condensed milk (milk-maid)

2 cups plain flour (*maida*), 1 tsp level soda-bi-carb

2 tsp level baking powder, 1¼ cups (180 gm) white butter - softened

½ cup powdered sugar, ½ cup cocoa powder, 1¼ cups (250 ml) milk

2 tbsp raisins, 4 tbsp sliced almonds, 1 tsp vanilla essence

TOPPING

50 gm chocolate, melted - as given on page 10

1. Grease and dust a big round cake tin of 10-11" diameter. Preheat oven to 150°C.
2. Sift maida, cocoa, soda-bi-carb and baking powder together. Keep aside.
3. Mix sugar and butter in a big bowl or a deep pan. Beat till very fluffy and light.
4. Add milk-maid and essence. Beat well to mix.
5. Add half of the flour. Add half of the milk. Mix well. Add the remaining milk and flour. Beat well for 3-4 minutes till the mixture is light and fluffy and you get a soft dropping consistency.

6. Mix the raisins with 1 tbsp flour to coat them. Add to the cake mixture. Transfer the cake batter to the tin.
7. Smoothen the top, pushing the mixture backwards from the centre to make a slight depression in the centre. This prevents forming of a peak!
8. Sprinkle almonds on top. Bake for 50-60 minutes in a pre-heated oven at 150°C. Check with a knife at the highest point of the cake. Remove from oven after 5 minutes.
9. Wait for another 5-10 minutes before removing from the tin on to the wire rack. Let it cool down.
10. Melt chocolate as given on page 10. Drizzle the chocolate with a spoon, going forwards and then backwards, covering the cake with chocolate lines. Keep outside the fridge till serving time.

Whole Wheat Honey Ginger Cake

Serves 10

¾ cup plain flour (*maida*), ½ cup whole wheat flour (*atta*), ¾ cup cocoa

¾ cup +2 tbsp regular sugar

¾ cup oil, ¼ cup honey

2-2½ tsp ground ginger powder (*sauth*)

3 large eggs, 1 tsp soda bi cab

1-2 tbsp crystallized ginger (preserved sweetened ginger pieces like glace cherries etc.) - chopped

1. Sieve both flours, cocoa, soda & ginger powder together. Keep aside.
2. Beat together eggs and sugar till sugar dissolves and mixture is frothy.
3. Add honey and oil. Beat for 2-3 minutes. Add chopped crystalized ginger.
4. Add flour little by little. Go on beating and adding flour to obtain a dropping consistency.
5. Pour into a greased 9" round tin. Put some thin ginger pieces on top also. Bake in a preheated oven at 150°C/300°F for 45 minutes or till the cake is done.

Chocolate Orange Cake

Makes 6-8 pieces

2 eggs
¼ cup yellow butter - softened, 1 cup powdered sugar
¼ cup orange squash, 1 tsp baking powder, ¼ cup cocoa
½ cup plain flour (*maida*), ¼ cup whole wheat flour (*atta*)
3-4 tbsp orange rind
2-3 segments of orange dipped in 25 gm melted chocolate

1. Beat butter and sugar till very soft and creamy.
2. Sift both flours with cocoa and baking powder and keep aside.
3. Add 1 egg to the butter-sugar mixture. Add half the flour also and mix. Add the other egg and the left over flour. Mix well.
4. Add orange rind and squash. Mix well to get a soft dropping consistency. Pour into a greased 8" square or round cake tin. Bake at 180°C for about 30 minutes or till done.
5. To decorate, melt 2-3 tbsp chopped chocolate for 30-45 seconds in a microwave till soft. Mix well till smooth. Dip orange segments in melted chocolate to coat the bottom and arrange on the cake.

Chocolate Truffle

Serves 14-16

1 quick chocolate cake of 4 eggs baked in an 8" square or a 9" round cake tin, pg 46
200 gms whipping cream, any tetra pack cream, discard liquid and use only thick cream

SUGAR SYRUP TO SOAK
¼ cup sugar and ¾ cup water

GANACHE FOR TRUFFLE ICING
200 gms cream, any tetra pack cream
300 gms dark cooking chocolate - chopped (3 cups)

1. Make a chocolate cake. Make sugar syrup by boiling water and sugar together. After the boil, keep syrup on low heat for 1 minute. Remove from heat and cool completely. Keep in the fridge.
2. To make ganache for truffle icing, heat 200 gms cream in a heavy bottom pan on low heat till it becomes hot. Do not let it boil. Add 300 gms chocolate to it. Mix nicely to remove any lumps. Remove from fire when almost melted and mix well. Let it cool. Keep aside.
3. Beat 200 gms whipping cream till stiff peaks form.

4. Mix about ½ cup ganache (chocolate-cream mixture) to the whipped cream to get a light brown chocolate cream. Keep chocolate cream in the fridge. Keep the remaining ganache aside for top coating, outside the fridge, so that the chocolate remains melted.

5. Thinly remove the top layer of the cake. Cut chocolate sponge into 3 layers.

6. Put the bottom layer on a plate, soak lightly with syrup. Spread ¼ of the prepared chocolate cream on it. Place the second sponge on it. Soak with 1/3 cup of syrup, using a spoon. Spread some chocolate cream on it. Place the top layer of cake on it. Again soak with 1/3 cup syrup.

7. Trim the sides. Cover the top and sides of the cake with the remaining chocolate cream. Keep it in the freezer for 15-20 minutes, till cream becomes firm.

8. Keep cake on a rack. Place a plate under the rack.

9. Check ganache. The ganache can be reheated with 1-2 tbsp water, if it has become too thick. It should be thin enough to flow properly. Pour the prepared ganache on the set cake and tilt rack to cover the sides of the cake also.

10. Decorate with chocolate sharts, as given below, on the sides, placing them a little higher than the cake at an angle and curved sticks on the top in the centre.

CHOCOLATE SHARTS (FLAT PIECES) AND CURVED STICKS
Melt 100 gm cooking chocolate in a double boiler as given on page 10

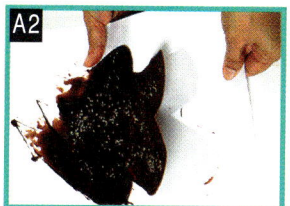

A. For sharts... (Make a few days ahead and store in a flat box in the chill tray)

   1. Spread half of the melted chocolate on butter paper/white paper in a thin layer with a palette knife or spatula as shown above. Quickly sprinkle with sesame seeds or grated white chocolate on it if you like. Keep in the freezer to set.

   2. Remove from freezer and peel off from the paper.

   3. Break into uneven shapes. Spread out on a plate and keep for 15 minutes in the chill tray to become hard. Arrange on the sides of the cake.

B. For curved sticks, see page 93. Fill remaining half of melted chocolate in a paper cone. Cut a slightly big tip. Squeeze out tall zig-zag lines on paper. Freeze and peel off.

Chocolate Tea Loaf

Serves 8-10

2 large eggs
80 gm (½ cup) butter, preferably white cooking butter
100 gm (1 cup) powdered sugar
½ tsp vanilla essence
75 gm (3/4 cup) plain flour (*maida*)
¼ cup plus 2 tbsp cocoa, 1 tsp level baking powder
½ cup mixed dry fruits (chopped walnuts, raisins, almonds, glace cherries)

1. Beat sugar and butter till light and fluffy. Beat till very creamy and smooth. Add essence. Mix.
2. Sift flour, cocoa and baking powder. Keep aside. Beat eggs till fluffy and keep aside.
3. Add half of the beaten eggs and half of the flour to the butter & sugar mixture. Beat. Repeat with left over flour and eggs. Beat for 3-4 minutes till mixture is light & fluffy.
4. Mix nuts with 1 tbsp flour. Add half of them to batter. Mix well with a spoon.
5. Put in a greased and dusted long, loaf tin. Sprinkle the remaining nuts on top. Make a slight depression in the centre with a spoon, by pushing the batter on the sides. Bake in preheated oven at 150°C/300°F for about 45 minutes or till done.

Toffee Cake

An eggless chocolate cake with a nutty toffee coating of jaggery.

Makes 10-12

1 cup flour (*maida*)
½ cup cocoa, ½ cup chopped walnuts
1 cup curd (use fresh curd), ¾ cup ordinary sugar
1½ tsp baking powder, ½ tsp soda bicarb (*mitha soda*)
½ cup oil, 1 tsp vanilla essence

TOFFEE SAUCE
1½ tbsp butter - softened, 4 tbsp jaggery (powdered gur)
4-6 tbsp fresh cream, 2 tbsp roughly chopped walnuts

1. Mix sugar and curd well. Stir till sugar dissolves completely.
2. Add baking powder and soda. Mix well. Keep aside for 3-4 minutes till bubbles start to appear.
3. Sieve the flour and cocoa. Mix walnuts with the flour. Keep aside.
4. Add oil to the curd mixture. Add essence. Mix well.
5. Lastly add the flour and mix well to get a thick but soft batter. Add a little more curd if the batter appears too thick and hard.
6. Transfer the mixture into a greased 9" loaf baking tin.
7. Bake in a preheated oven at 210°C for 10 minutes. Reduce heat to 150°C and bake further for 20-25 minutes or until done. Test with a knife to see that it comes out clean. Remove from oven after 5 minutes.
8. Let the cake cool in the tin for 10 minutes and then remove from tin on a wire rack.
9. For the sauce, heat butter in a small thick bottomed sauce pan on medium heat. Add the jaggery. Cook for 1 minute till the mixture is frothy. Remove from heat. Add the cream. Return to low heat. Stir for a few seconds till well blended. Do not bring to a boil. Add the walnuts.
10. Remove from fire and pour over the cake.

Swirled Ring Cake

This method of swirling converts a simple cake into a perfect treat.

Serves 16

4 eggs
150 gm (1½ cups) flour, 1½ tsp baking powder
150 gm (1½ cups) powdered sugar
¾ cup oil
2 tsp vanilla essence
5 tbsp Cadbury's drinking chocolate powder
¼ cup hot water

1. Grease an 8" ring tin or a round tin.
2. Sift flour and baking powder together.
3. Separate eggs.
4. Beat egg whites in clean dry bowl till thick and fluffy.
5. Add sugar gradually, beating till thick and retains shape.
6. Beat in essence and yolk till thick and retains shape.
7. Add oil, very gradually beating till thick again.
8. Fold in flour gently with wooden or metal spoon.
9. Mix chocolate powder with hot water to get a thick paste.
10. Add this chocolate paste to cake mixture with a spoon and gently swirl with another spoon to make marble effect. Do not use the same spoon for marbling and also do not mix uniformly. Both vanilla and chocolate mixture should show separately as marble effect.
11. Pour mixture into tin and bake in preheated oven at 160°C for 35-40 minutes.
12. Insert skewer or knife in the centre of cake, if it comes out clean remove tin from oven. Transfer to wire rack after 5 minutes and cool.
13. Transfer to a platter and sprinkle the platter with a few pinches of drinking chocolate. You can decorate the platter with a squeeze of ready-made chocolate sauce too.

Choco Orange Mousse Cake

Chocolate and orange make a mouth watering combination in this creamy mousse cake.

Serves 16

quick chocolate cake baked in 10"-11" loose bottom round tin, pg 46

MOUSSE
400 gms cream (tetra pack), 6 tsp gelatine, ¾ cup orange juice
¼ cup powdered sugar, or to taste, 1 tsp orange essence
2 tbsp orange crush or marmalade, few drops orange colour
75 gm cooking chocolate/bournville chocolate - chopped (¾ cup)

ASSEMBLING OF MOUSSE CAKE
½ cup orange juice, or as required
1 orange
some fresh pomegranate (*anaar*)

1. For the mousse, sprinkle gelatine over orange juice. Keep aside for 5 minutes.
2. Melt chocolate in a double boiler as given on page 10.
3. Beat cream. Put 2 tbsp sugar from the measured amount and beat till slightly thick. Add the remaining sugar and beat till soft peaks form. Add essence.
4. Dissolve gelatine on low heat. Do not boil. Remove from fire.
5. Add some cream into the gelatine mix. Add this mix into the remaining cream very slowly, mixing well. Divide the mixture into 2 portions.
6. Add the melted chocolate to one portion of the cream. Check sugar.
7. To the other part, add orange marmalade or crush. Add colour.
8. Cut the cake into 2 round pieces, each of 1" thickness. Place one base sponge at the bottom of the loose bottom tin. Press. Sprinkle lightly with orange juice. Pour the orange mousse mixture on it. Put the other layer of sponge on it. Soak the cake with juice. Pour the chocolate mixture on it. Keep in the freezer for about 1-2 hours or till it sets well.
9. When set, demould mousse cake on platter. Arrange oranges and fresh pomegranate on the sides.

Wild Strawberry Passion

Serves 8

1 cup flour (*maida*), ¼ cup cornflour, ½ cup cocoa
1½ tsp baking powder, ¾ tsp soda-bi-carb
¾ cup white butter (100 gm), ¾ cup powdered sugar
1 cup milk, ½ tsp vanilla essence
20 gm dark chocolate or milk chocolate - cut into small pieces
4 tbsp milk

GLAZED STRAWBERRIES
200 gm (1 packet) strawberries - cut into slices, 4 tbsp fruit jam

SOAKING SYRUP
¾ cup water, 1½ tbsp sugar, 1 tsp coffee, 1 tsp vanilla essence
½ cup chocolate sauce (ready made)

1. Sift flour, cornflour, cocoa, baking powder and soda-bi-carb.
2. Beat butter and sugar till fluffy. Add flour mixture and 1 cup milk. Mix.
3. Cut chocolate into small pieces. Put with 4 tbsp milk in a clean, heavy bottomed kadhai on very low heat. When it just starts to melt, remove from fire and mix well with a rubber spatula till it melts properly and turns glossy.
4. Add melted chocolate and essence to the cake batter. Beat till fluffy. Bake in a greased 7-8" diameter cake tin at 180°C for 30-35 minutes. Remove from oven and let it cool.
5. For the strawberries, mix 2-3 tbsp water and 4 tbsp jam in a pan. Stirring continuously, cook on low heat till jam melts. Reduce heat to minimum. Add strawberry slices to the syrup and stir gently for a few seconds till well coated and glazed. Remove the glazed strawberries to a plate.
6. For the soaking syrup, boil water and sugar. Add coffee and remove from fire. Add essence. Let it cool down.
7. Place the cake in a serving platter with the bottom side on top. Soak it with coffee syrup till very moist. Pour chocolate sauce on it. Spread to cover the top nicely till the edges. Let it drip from the sides.
8. Arrange slices of strawberry on the cake, starting from the outer edge. Place the next row slightly overlapping the first. Make the centre slices sit a little upright. Keep in the refrigerator. Cut into wedges to serve.

Tea Time Treats

Tea Time Treats

Chocolate Muffins

Makes 8

1½ cups flour (*maida*), ¼ cup + 1 tbsp cocoa
1½ tsp baking powder, ¾ tsp soda-bi-carb
½ cup butter - softened, 1 cup powdered sugar
1 cup milk, 3 tbsp chocolate - cut into small pieces (chips)
2 tbsp raisins (*kishmish*)

1. Sieve the flour, cocoa, baking powder and the soda-bi-carb.
2. Beat butter and sugar till light and fluffy.
3. Add the flour and milk. Mix well.
4. Add kishmish and 2 tbsp chocolate chips to the cake batter.
5. Pour into small cake moulds or small steel *katoris* which are lightly greased with oil. If you like, place paper cups in the moulds.
6. Sprinkle chocolate chips on top.
7. Bake at 180°C/350°F for 20 minutes till golden and the cake shrinks from the sides of the tins.

Choco Web Pie

For a good short crust base it is important to chill the unbaked crust in the freezer for 10-15 minutes and then put in the hot oven. The pastry is much lighter this way.

Makes 16 thin pieces

SHORT CRUST
1½ cups (150 gm) plain flour (*maida*)
5 bread slices - grind in a mixer to get 2½ cups fresh bread crumbs
100 gm butter - cut into pieces and keep in the fridge to chill
3 tbsp powdered sugar

CARAMEL NUT FILLING
1 cup roasted peanuts, ½ cup raisins (*kishmish*)
½ cup almonds - chopped and roasted in a pan till fragrant and light golden
1¼ cups grain sugar, 1/3 cup water
¾ cup cream - at room temperature

GANACHE TOPPING
200 gm chocolate - chopped, 150 gm cream (¾ cup), 1 tbsp rum (optional)

TO DECORATE
16 cherries, some chocolate curls, see page 93

1. Put cold butter in a mixer with sugar and churn for a few seconds. Add flour and fresh bread crumbs to the mixer and run mixer for a few seconds till the mixture turns crumbly. Remove from mixer. Collect mixture together and mix gently into a dough of rolling consistency. Wrap in a cling wrap. Keep aside for 30 minutes in the fridge.

2. Grease a 8-9" flan tin or pie tin.

3. Roll out a large chappati, larger than the tin so as to cover the sides too, of 1/8" thickness. Rolling dough between 2 sheets of polythene makes it easier to roll.

4. Place in the flan tin. Prick with a fork. Neatly trim sides, keeping the sides to a height of ¾". Do not make the pie too high.

5. Keep in the freezer for 10 minutes. Bake blind for 20 minutes at 200°C till light golden. Keep the baked pie crust or shell aside to cool.

6. For the caramel nut topping, measure ¾ cup cream at room temperature and keep aside. Put ¾ cup sugar in a flat non stick bottom pan in a thin layer. Let it turn golden on the edges without stirring. Lift the pan and rotate the pan to melt the sugar evenly and turn golden. Add cream. Mix well. Return to fire.

7. Add ¼ cup warm water and stir continuously to dissolve the lump. Do not lift the lumpy spoon from the pan as the caramelized sugar turns hard and it becomes difficult to dissolve the lump. Keep stirring on low heat till smooth. Let it cool to room temperature. Add almonds, raisins and peanuts. Mix well. Fill nuts into the cooled pie crust or shell.

8. For the ganache topping, warm cream on low heat in a heavy pan for 1 minute. Add chocolate. Mix well. Remove from heat and stir well to get a smooth ganache. Add 1 tbsp rum. Mix. Pour over the nuts to cover completely.

9. Refrigerate for 1-2 hours to set. Mark circles with a tooth pick at ½" gaps. Similarly, mark lines from the centre to the edge of the pie at ½" distance to get a web effect. Arrange almonds and curls on the pie. Serve pie cold or at room temperature.

Walnut Brownies

Makes 10

100 gm white butter (2/3 cup)
1½ cups brown sugar
2 eggs
1 tsp vanilla essence
½ cup flour (*maida*)
¼ tsp baking powder
½ cup cocoa
¾ cup walnuts - cut into small pieces or crushed roughly with a rolling pin
some chocolate sauce, optional

1. Melt butter in a heavy deep pan on low heat. Add brown sugar. Mix well with a wooden spoon on low heat for 2-3 minutes till well blended.
2. Remove from fire. Wait for a minute for the mixture to cool slightly. Add one egg. Mix well with a wooden spoon. Add the second egg and mix again. Add essence.
3. Sift flour, baking powder and cocoa together.
4. Keeping aside ¼ cup walnuts, add the rest of the walnuts to the flour and mix well with the hands.
5. Mix the flour mixture in the butter-egg mixture very gently with a wooden spoon.
6. Grease a 7"-8" square tin. Transfer the cake mixture in it to get 1" thick layer of the mixture. Sprinkle the remaining walnuts.
7. Bake for about 30 minutes at 160°C or till done. Cool. Cut into squares in the tin itself to get neat pieces. Remove pieces with a flat spoon.
8. Warm in a microwave to serve.

Chocolate Donuts

Makes 10 medium size donuts

1½ cups plain flour (*maida*), 1 egg
2 tsp dry yeast, ¼ cup warm water + ½ tsp sugar
¼ cup powdered sugar
milk as required to knead
1 tbsp butter - softened

GLACE ICING FOR COATING
200 gm icing sugar
3-4 tbsp hot water, 7 tbsp cocoa powder
1 tbsp yellow butter, 1 tsp vanilla essence

1. Mix ½ tsp sugar to ¼ cup warm water. Add yeast and cover the cup. Invert an empty deep pan on the cup to keep it warm. Wait for 15 minutes till it rises and gets frothy. If it does not rise, discard it and start with a fresh packet of yeast.

2. Put flour, egg and sugar in a bowl. Add the frothy yeast and mix well. Knead into a soft dough using some milk if required.

3. Add softened butter and knead again till the dough is smooth and elastic. (3-5 minutes).

4. Put in a greased polythene. Cover with an inverted empty deep pan again and keep in a warm place to swell. (½ hour). Once the dough rises, punch down the dough. Knead again for 10 minutes.

5. Roll out dough to ¼" thickness. Cut out 3" diameter circles with a cookie cutter or a bottle lid. Using a tiny cookie cutter or a very small lid, cut out the centre of each round, to create a hole in the centre. Make such donuts and cover with a wet muslin cloth for 5-10 minutes.

6. To fry - heat fresh oil in a kadahi. Reduce heat. Deep fry 2-3 pieces at a time on low heat till golden on both sides.

7. For the chocolate glaze, sift the icing sugar. Put cocoa in a stainless steel bowl. Add boiling hot water to cocoa and mix well. Add icing sugar and butter. Boil 1" water in a small saucepan. Reduce heat. Place the bowl of icing sugar on it. Melt sugar, stirring occasionally. Remove from fire.

8. Dip one side of the donut in it and place on a plate lined with aluminium sheet with the chocolate side up. Cool till chocolate sets.

Chocolate Swiss Rolls

Servings 12

CAKE
1 baking tray - size 9"x11" approx. (swiss roll tray)
4 large eggs, ½ cup flour (*maida*), 3 tbsp cocoa powder
½ cup plus 2 tbsp powdered sugar, 2 level tsp baking powder
1 tsp vanilla essence

CHOCOLATE FILLING
½ cup white butter - softened
¾ cup icing sugar - sifted, ¼ cup cocoa, approx, 1 tsp vanilla essence

COATING
some powdered sugar or chocolate coating as for eclairs see page 75, step 11

1. Separate white and yolk of eggs. Beat egg whites in a dry pan, till stiff.
2. Gradually add sugar to egg whites, beating after each addition. Gently add yolks and mix lightly.
3. Sift flour, cocoa with baking powder.
4. Add flour to eggs & fold gently with a spoon. Add essence. Do not over mix. Pour into a greased and dusted rectangular baking tray. Tilt the tray to spread mixture uniformly. Bake for 15 minutes in a preheated oven at 200°C. When the cake leaves the sides of the tray and is springy to touch, remove from oven.
5. Spread 1 tbsp powdered sugar on a grease proof paper or aluminium foil and turn out the cake over the sugar. Roll the cake along with the paper. Let it cool down completely before spreading the filling.
6. To prepare the filling, sift sugar & cocoa powder. In a pan put softened butter. Beat till fluffy. Add all the other ingredients and beat well till well mixed. (Add more cocoa and sugar, according to your taste.)
7. Spread the chocolate filling on the cool cake and roll forwards. Pack roll tightly in aluminium foil and keep in the fridge for 2-3 hours.
8. If you like a chocolate topping, do as given on page 75 for eclairs (step 11). Pour chocolate in the centre along the length of the roll. Let it drizzzle on the sides. Let the chocolate dry. To serve, cut the roll into 10-12 pieces with a sharp knife.

Mocha Petit Fours

The combined flavour of coffee, chocolate and butterscotch make these little pastries very exciting and delicious.

Makes 20

1 quick chocolate cake baked in a 9" square tin, p 46

CREAM ICING
300 gm (1½ cups) cream, ½ cup icing sugar, 2 tsp butter scotch essence

COFFEE SYRUP TO SOAK
¾ cup water, ¼ cup powdered sugar
2 tsp coffee, 1 tsp butterscotch essence

OTHER INGREDIENTS
100 gm cooking chocolate - at room temp.
2 tsp coffee powder mixed with 2 tsp water

1. Make a chocolate cake in a big square tin of about 9"-10" in size. Cut into two horizontally when it cools. Cover both pieces and keep aside.

2. Get the chocolate at room temperature (neither chilled nor melting) to get big curls. Scrape the side of a chocolate slab with a peeler to get smooth curls. Press the peeler hard as you peel along, to get proper curls. Make 20 chocolate curls and keep in the freezer to become stiff. Cut the rest of the chocolate into pieces.

3. Microwave the chopped chocolate pieces in a bowl for 1 minute. Mix well to make it smooth.

4. For the icing, beat cream till slightly thick. Add icing sugar and essence. Beat till soft peaks form. Add 1 cup of whipped cream to melted chocolate to get choco-cream. To the remaining cream, add 2 tsp coffee mixed with water to get coffee cream.

5. Mix ¾ cup water, sugar, coffee & essence. Soak the bottom layer of cake. Spread choco-cream. Cover with the other piece of cake. Soak lightly again. Cut cake into 2" squares.

6. Cover each piece with coffee-cream. To decorate, top with a chocolate curl.

Chocolate Eclairs

Makes 12

CHOUX PASTRY
75 gm plain flour (*maida*), a pinch of salt, 25 gm (2 tbsp) butter or margarine

¾ cup (140 ml) water

1 tsp sugar (optional), 2 eggs

FILLING
200 gm cream

4 tbsp icing sugar - sifted

¼ tsp vanilla essence

CHOCOLATE COATING
100 gm (½ cup) fresh cream

150 gm dark cooking chocolate-chopped

1 tsp butter

1. To prepare the choux pastry, sift flour and salt together.

2. Put butter, water and sugar into a sauce pan and heat gently until butter melts; then raise the heat and rapidly bring mixture to boil.

3. Remove the pan from fire and add all the flour at once. Stir quickly with a wooden spoon until flour absorbs all liquid. Return to heat and stir until a smooth ball is formed and it leaves the sides of the pan. Allow the mixture to cool a little.

4. Beat eggs till fluffy. Gradually mix eggs and beat till the eggs are well mixed. The choux pastry should be thick enough to hold its shape but not stiff.

5. Spoon pastry into a stiff (transparent) polythene bag. Cut one corner to pipe ½" thick fingers.

6. Pipe out 2" long fingers on a greased baking tray. Start piping with the cut end touching the tray and lifting it while pressing the mixture out, cut off the required length with a wet knife.

Contd...

7. Place hot oven at 220°C/425°F & bake for about 20 minutes, until crisp and golden brown. (If eclairs are not thoroughly dry, reduce the heat to 180°C/350°F and continue baking for further 10 minutes).

8. Remove from the oven. Slit them down on one side to let the steam escape and leave on a wire rack to cool.

9. Beat the chilled cream and sugar till it forms soft peaks. Cool in the fridge.

10. When eclairs are cold, fill them with whipped cream using a piping bag and a nozzle. Keep in fridge.

11. To prepare the top icing, break softened chocolate into small pieces. Heat the cream in a small heavy bottomed pan, on low heat (do not boil). Add chocolate pieces and heat stirring continuously, till chocolate melts & you get an almost smooth paste. Remove from fire and stir in butter gently till it turns smooth. Immediately pour over the eclairs to cover the top completely. Keep under refrigeration for 2-3 hours till the icing sets.

Choco Truffle Tarts

> *Makes 10*

3-4 tbsp chopped walnuts

SHORT CRUST PASTRY (DOUGH) FOR TART SHELLS
200 gm plain flour (2¼ cups *maida*)
100 gm salted butter - cold, a pinch baking powder
2 tbsp powdered sugar, 3-4 tbsp ice cold water

CHOCOLATE BUTTER ICING
1 cup white butter - softened, 1½ cups icing sugar - sifted
½ cup cocoa, can add more if desired, 1 tsp vanilla essence

TRUFFLE FILLING
120 gm chocolate - chopped, ½ cup cream

1. Cut the cold, solid butter into small pieces.
2. Add baking powder, sugar and butter to the flour. Rub the butter into the flour with the finger tips till it resembles bread crumbs.
3. Add 2-3 tbsp cold water. Bind into a dough of rolling consistency. Knead lightly.
4. Roll out large chappati of 1/8" thickness. Cut out small circles with a biscuit cutter or *katori*, which is slightly bigger than the tart mould and fit them into tart tins. Prick with a fork. Keep in the freezer for 10 minutes. Bake empty (blind) for 8 minutes in the centre of a hot oven at 200°C till very light golden in colour. Take out from oven. Cool.
5. To prepare the chocolate butter icing, whip butter till smooth. Mix all the other ingredients and beat till well blended. Transfer to a piping bag and keep in the refrigerator.
6. For the truffle filling, heat cream on low heat. Add chocolate. Stir for 2 minutes, continuously on low heat. Do not let it boil. Remove from heat when smooth and glossy. Cool to room temperature.
7. To fill the tart shell, pipe chocolate butter icing at the edges, along the tart shell. Drop a spoonful of truffle filling in the centre to fill the empty space. Sprinkle some chopped walnuts on the sides. Refrigerate till serving time.

Chocolate Chip Cookies

Mix chocolate bits into the cookie dough & bake – children will love these cookies & will love to make them too!

Makes 12-15

60 gm white butter, softened
3 tbsp castor sugar, ½ tsp vanilla essence
1 cup flour (*maida*), 2 tbsp rice flour or cornflour, ½ tsp baking powder
60 gm dark chocolate - chopped

1. Beat the butter and sugar very well until light and creamy. Beating at this step has to be done very well. The more you beat, the better it is. Add the vanilla essence and beat again.
2. Sieve the flour, rice flour and baking powder.
3. Add the flour and chocolate pieces to the butter. Gently mix to get a soft dough. Do not knead, just gather ingredients together to make a very soft dough.
4. Shape into small rounds. Flatten to make cookies.
5. Cover the back of a baking tray with aluminium foil and grease it with butter. Place cookies 1" apart. Bake in a preheated oven at 180°C/350°F for 15-20 min.

Pinwheel Biscuits

Cocoa and vanilla are made for each other – enjoy them together in these quick and easy-to-make biscuits.

Makes 16

240 gm (2½ cups) flour (*maida*)
1 tsp baking powder, 1/8 tsp salt
130 gm butter (¾ cup approx.)
120 gm (slightly less than 1 cup) powdered sugar
½ tsp vanilla essence
3 tbsp milk
3 tbsp cocoa powder

1. Sieve flour, baking powder and salt together.
2. Cream butter and powdered sugar till light and fluffy.
3. Add the flour, vanilla essence and milk. Mix gently to make a stiff dough.
4. Divide the mixture into two parts and blend cocoa powder in one part.
5. Thinly roll out both the doughs to 1/8" thickness into equal sized pieces.
6. Place the chocolate piece on top of the white one. Roll the two tightly as for swiss rolls and allow to stand in a cool place for 20-30 minutes.
7. Cut into ¼" thick slices and place on a well greased baking tray.
8. Bake in a moderate oven at 180°C/350°F for about 10-15 minutes.

Double Choc Fudge Cake

A baked dark chocolate fudge cake topped with white chocolate layer which is set in the refrigerator. Once the topping is set, the cake can be kept upto a week or 10 days. Tastes best when served at room temperature, so take it out of the fridge an hour before serving.

Serves 16-20

85 gm white butter
200 gm dark cooking chocolate - chopped finely
220 gm powdered sugar, 3 eggs, beaten lightly
100 gm flour, ¼ cup cocoa, ½ tsp baking powder

WHITE CHOCOLATE FUDGE
250 gm white chocolate - chopped fine
100 cup thick cream (½ cup), 1½ tbsp amaretto or brandy

MARBLE CHOCOLATE CURLS
100 gm dark cooking chocolate, 50 gm white cooking chocolate

1. Line the base of a 8" round loose bottom cake tin with foil. Grease foil and put it in the tin. Grease sides of the tin too. Keep aside.

2. Melt butter on low heat in a deep sauce pan, stir in dark chocolate and mix over low heat for 1-2 minutes till smooth. Remove from heat. Let it cool completely.

3. Stir in sugar gradually. Mix well. Add eggs, mix well. If the chocolate is warm, the eggs will start to cook!

4. Sift flour, baking powder and cocoa together. Mix in sifted flour, baking powder and cocoa, until well combined to get a thickish batter. Spread over base of tin.

5. Bake in pre-heated oven at 180°C for 45 minutes. Insert skewer to check if done and remove cake from oven. Let it cool completely.

6. For white chocolate fudge layer, warm cream in a heavy bottomed pan over low heat. Add white chocolate, cook stirring for about 2-3 minutes until chocolate melts to a very thick pouring consistency. Cool and add brandy.

7. After the chocolate cake cools down completely, put it back in the tin. Pour the white chocolate fudge on the dark chocolate cake in the tin. Spread to cover cake. Refrigerate for 4-5 hours until set. Decorate with marble curls as given on the next page. Remove from fridge 1-2 hours before serving. Serve at room temperature, cut into very thin slices.

Contd...

MARBLE CHOCOLATE CURLS FOR FUDGE CAKE

1. To decorate with curls, melt 100 gm dark cooking chocolate in double boiler, (see page 10) Heat 1" water in deep sauce pan. Place chocolate in another pan which covers the 1st pan but does not touch the water. Do not stir chocolate till the chocolate becomes soft and starts to melt on its own. Stir gently to melt the chocolate into a smooth paste.

2. Pour half of this mixture on a clean kitchen slab and spread with a knife to 1/8" thickness. Leave the dark chocolate to cool.

3. Soften white chocolate also on the double boiler or in a microwave for 1 minute, stir with a spoon till it melts. Add the melted white chocolate to the remaining dark chocolate. Do not stir.

4. Pour this separately on the slab and spread to 1/8" thickness. Cool.

5. Hold a sharp broad blade knife on the cooled dark chocolate layer, press and move along chocolate to take out curls.

6. Make curls in similar way from the set layer of marbled chocolate.

7. Lay marbled chocolate curls around the cake. Place dark chocolate curls in the middle.

Chocolate Desserts

Chocolate Desserts

Dark Chocolate Mousse

A simple bowl of fabulously rich, silken chocolate mousse!

Serves 8

5 large egg yolks
½ cup sugar
1/3 cup water
200 gm dark chocolate - finely chopped
200 gm (1 cup) heavy cream, chilled
some ready made chocolate sauce, optional

1. Drizzle chocolate sauce on the sides of a serving bowl and keep in the refrigerator.
2. Whisk the egg yolks and sugar in a large heat proof bowl on hot water placed in a double boiler. Make a double boiler as you make one for melting the chocolate as given on page 10. Whisk together for about 4-5 minutes, until the mixture turns pale yellow and thick, and the sugar begins to dissolve.
3. Stir in the water. Continue whisking vigorously until the mixture is quite thick and coats the back of a spoon.
4. Remove from the heat and add the finely chopped chocolate. Stir until melted. Continue stirring until the mixture is cool to touch.
5. In a separate bowl, whisk the cream until soft peaks form. Gently fold cream into the melted chocolate mixture.
6. Transfer to the prepared serving bowl. Cover and refrigerate for about 4 hours.
7. To decorate with chocolate leaves spread melted chocolate on the shiny upper side of a clean Ficus leaf. Leave to dry on a plate lined with aluminium foil. Keep in the fridge in hot weather.
8. Very carefully peel the leaf off the chocolate, starting at the stem end. Keep in the fridge to firm up for about 2-3 hours. Arrange on the dessert.

Striped Chocolate Cheese Cake

A beautiful white and chocolate striped cheese cake.

Serves 12

BISCUIT BASE

24 chocolate chip biscuits

7 tbsp melted butter

CHEESE CAKE

4½ cups curd - hang for 2 hours in a thin muslin cloth

125 gm butter (¾ cup) - softened

1¾ cups powdered sugar

3 tbsp gelatine

2 tsp lemon juice

100 gms dark chocolate - chopped (1 cup)

1. Place the biscuits in a plastic bag and crush the biscuits with a rolling pin to a coarse powder.

2. Mix in melted butter with finger tips. Take 2-3 tbsp of mixture in the hand and press with the fingers to check if it binds together. Add 1 tbsp milk if required to bind the biscuits.

3. Press into the base of an 8" loose bottomed cake tin with the help of small bowl with a flat bottom. (The loose bottom tin allows you to unmould the cheese cake with the biscuit base intact). Press the buttered crumbs evenly and firmly onto the bottom of the pan

4. Bake in a pre-heated oven at 180°C/350°F for 10 minutes. Keep aside.

5. Beat butter till smooth. Add hung curd and sugar. Beat well.

6. Soak the gelatine in ¼ cup water. Heat on a low fire until dissolved. Add 2 tsp lemon juice

7. Add gelatine gradually to the curd mixture, stirring well after each addition. Mix well.

8. Divide the mixture into two parts.

9. Cut the chocolate into small pieces. Melt over a double boiler. Remove from fire and stir gently till smooth.

10. Add ½ of the melted chocolate to one cheese cake mixture, keeping the other mixture white. Leave the remaining chocolate mixture outside on hot water

11. Pour the chocolate curd mixture on the biscuit base in the tin. Keep the white mixture aside.

12. Chill chocolate cheese cake for ½ hour in the freezer to firm up.

13. Remove from freezer. Pour remaining white mixture (whip it if it sets) on top of the chocolate mixture and now chill in the refrigerator. (Do not keep in the freezer).

14. After 1 hour, when the top layer of the cheese cake is set, pour the left over melted chocolate over the cheese cake. Serve after 3-4 hours or after it is set.

Chocolate Freezer Cake

A fatless chocolate sponge cake made in a ring tin and filled with ice cream and frozen.

Serves 8

4 eggs, ¾ cup powdered sugar, a pinch of salt

½ cup flour (*maida*), ¼ cup cocoa

1 tsp baking powder

2¼ cups chocolate and mint ice cream

50 gms dark chocolate - melted as given on page 10

9" ring pan or ring mould

1. To line the ring mould invert till on paper and cut out the paper. Place paper on the tin and mark centre. Cut out the centre. Line the tin with the paper strip and grease it well.

2. Place the eggs and sugar in a large mixing bowl. Add a pinch of salt. Using an electric mixer, beat the mixture until it is very thick and frothy. Stand the bowl over a smaller pan of hot water while beating. See that the bottom of the bowl does not touch the hot water.

3. Sift the flour, cocoa and baking powder together and add to the egg mixture. Do not beat. Using a wooden spoon, gently fold the maida mixture into the frothy eggs, with an upward and downward motion of the spoon. Mix well but gently.

4. Pour cake mixture into the prepared tin. Bake in a preheated oven, 350°F/ 180°C, for 20 minutes or until springy to the touch. Let cool in the pan before turning out on to a wire rack to cool completely.

5. Rinse the empty cake tin and line the bottom and the sides of the tin with a large piece of plastic wrap or foil, such that it is more in height and is overhanging slightly.

6. Carefully cut off the top ½ inch/1 cm of the cake in one slice, and then set aside.

7. Return the cake to the pan. Using a spoon, scoop out the centre of the cake, leaving a border or a shell of about ½ inch thick all around - outer and inner circle.

8. Remove the ice cream from the freezer and let stand for a few minutes, then beat with a wooden spoon until softened a little.

9. Fill the centre of the cake with the ice cream, carefully smoothing the top.

10. Replace the top of the cake. Cover with the overhanging plastic wrap and freeze the cake for at least 2 hours. To serve, turn the chocolate freezer cake out onto a serving dish and drizzle over some of the melted chocolate in an attractive pattern, if wished. Cut the cake into slices and the serve the remaining chocolate sauce separately.

Chocolate Marquis

The Marquis, a perfectly smooth, frozen mousse, is a classic French restaurant dessert. It cuts beautifully into very thin slices.

Serves 12

5 eggs, separated
½ cup + 2 tablespoons sugar
½ cup water
300 gm dark chocolate - finely chopped
100 gm unsalted butter - at room temperature, 200 gm (1 cup) heavy cream - chilled
9"-10" loose bottom cake tin or 12 small tart pans for individual servings

1. Whisk the egg yolks and ¼ cup sugar in a large heat proof bowl on hot water placed in a double boiler. Make a double boiler as you make one for melting the chocolate as given on page 10. Whisk together for about 4-5 minutes, until the mixture turns pale yellow and thick, and the sugar begins to dissolve.

2. Stir in the remaining ¼ cup water. Continue whisking vigorously for about 2-3 minutes, until the mixture is quite thick and foamy.

3. Remove the egg yolk-sugar mixture from the double boiler. Add the finely chopped chocolate. Stir until melted. Continue stirring until cool to the touch.

4. Stir in the softened butter. Set aside.

5. In a separate bowl whisk the cream until soft peaks form. Chill in the refrigerator.

6. In a small heavy saucepan combine the remaining sugar (¼ cup + 2 tbsp) with the remaining ¼ cup water. Cook over medium heat, stirring until the sugar is dissolved and the mixture is clear. Increase the heat to high and boil, without stirring, until it thickens and large bubbles form, about a minute.

7. Meanwhile, whip the egg whites until soft, glossy peaks form. With the mixer running, add the boiling sugar syrup in a slow, steady stream. Continue whipping until the peaks are stiff but not dry and the mixture feels luke warm to touch.

8. Quickly fold ¼ portion of beaten whites into the chocolate mixture. Then gently fold in the remaining whites in three parts, trying not to over mix.

9. Fold whipped cream also in 3 parts, gently folding until you can no longer see any streaks of white. Transfer to rinsed loose bottom tin. Level with a rubber spatula. Cover with aluminium foil and keep in the freezer for 4 hours atleast. Transfer to a serving platter. Decorate with chocolate nets as given on page 93.

Chocolate Decorations

The decorations have to be chilled after they are made so that they can be handled comfortably. The decorations when refrigerated for a few hours, become firm and do not melt while they are being placed on the cakes or desserts.

Making Scrolls

Melt chocolate in a double boiler as given on page 10. Thinly spread melted chocolate as smoothly as possible on a clean flat surface (kitchen platform) and leave to set. Place the knife at the far end. Firmly place the knife at a slight angle on the chocolate. Push knife from both ends to carefully scrape the chocolate off in long scrolls as shown above. Chill and decorate on a cake as shown.

Chocolate Leaves

Spread melted chocolate on the shiny upper side of a clean leaf. Leave to dry on a plate lined with aluminium foil. Keep in the fridge in hot weather.

Very carefully peel the leaf off the chocolate, starting at the stem end. Keep chocolate leaves in the fridge till required.

Decorate cakes or desserts with chocolate leaves. Rose & Ficus leaves work best.

Making Curls

Get the chocolate at room temperature (neither chilled nor melting) to get big curls. Scrape the side of a chocolate slab with a peeler to get smooth curls. Press the peeler hard as you peel along, to get proper curls.

Chocolate Nets & Sticks

A. For nets, draw crisscross lines on any paper. Make a cone with butter paper. Secure cone with scotch tape. Put melted white chocolate or dark chocolate in the cone. Cut out a slightly big tip. Pipe chocolate on the drawn lines on the paper. Freeze paper for 5 minutes. Peel off the paper carefully to take out nets from paper. Keep nets for atleast 1 hour in the freezer on a plate to become hard and firm. Arrange on cakes and desserts.

B V. For curved sticks, fill melted chocolate in a paper cone. Cut out a slightly big tip. Squeeze out tall zig-zag lines on paper. Freeze paper and peel off.

Chocolate Sharts
(Flat chocolate pieces placed on the sides)
. *(Make a few days ahead and store in a flat box in the chill tray)*

1. Melt 100 gm cooking chocolate in a double boiler as given on page 10. Spread melted chocolate on butter paper/white paper in a thin layer with a palette knife or a rubber spatula as shown below. Quickly sprinkle with sesame seeds or grate white chocolate on it if you like. Keep paper in the freezer to set.
2. Remove from freezer and peel off from the paper.
3. Break into uneven shapes. Spread out on a plate and keep for 30 minutes in the chill tray to become hard. Arrange on the sides of the cake.

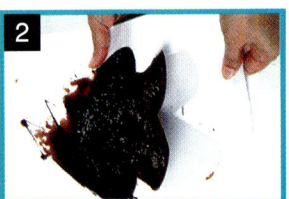

Glossary

Amaretto, liqueur	Almond-flavoured liqueur
Baking Powder	A raising agent consisting of 2 parts cream of tartar to 1 part bicarbonate soda. It is effected by heat and moisture and reacts to produce carbon dioxide gas, which is trapped within the protein structure of the product which is being baked.
Bicarbonate of Soda	Is also known in some countries as baking soda. It is usually used as a raising agent for cakes, pastries and breads.
Brown Sugar	Is a coarse crystal sugar and as the natural colouring of the raw sugar has not been removed, it retains its light brown colour. Also called Demerara sugar.
Castor Sugar	Very finely granulated table sugar. You can grind granulated sugar at home and use as castor sugar. It dissolves quickly when creamed with butter.
Cointreau, liqueur	Citrus-flavoured liqueur
Corn syrup	Available light or dark, liquid glucose can be substituted.
Cream	Milk fat. Single cream has 18% fat content, whipping cream has 38% fat and double cream 48% fat.
Crème de Cacao, liqueur	Chocolate-flavour liqueur
Demerara Sugar	Is a coarse crystal sugar and as the natural colouring of the raw sugar has not been removed, it retains its light brown colour. Also called brown sugar.
Food Colourings	Available in liquid, powder or paste form.
Icing Sugar	Also known as confectioners sugar. Superfine granulated sugar with addition of 3% cornflour. Used mainly for icing cakes and pastries. Icing sugar gives a softer finish when dusted over the top of cakes and biscuits.
Kahlua, Liqueur	Coffee-flavoured liqueur
Kirsch, Liqueur	Cherry-flavoured liqueur
Whipping Cream	Is a lighter version of double cream, with at least 35% fat content and whips easily without the richness. Excellent as a pouring cream or for swirling on desserts.

INTERNATIONAL CONVERSION GUIDE

These are not exact equivalents; they've been rounded-off to make measuring easier.

WEIGHTS & MEASURES

METRIC	IMPERIAL
15 g	½ oz
30 g	1 oz
60 g	2 oz
90 g	3 oz
125 g	4 oz (¼ lb)
155 g	5 oz
185 g	6 oz
220 g	7 oz
250 g	8 oz (½ lb)
280 g	9 oz
315 g	10 oz
345 g	11 oz
375 g	12 oz (¾ lb)
410 g	13 oz
440 g	14 oz
470 g	15 oz
500 g	16 oz (1 lb)
750 g	24 oz (1½ lb)
1 kg	30 oz (2 lb)

LIQUID MEASURES

METRIC	IMPERIAL
30 ml	1 fluid oz
60 ml	2 fluid oz
100 ml	3 fluid oz
125 ml	4 fluid oz
150 ml	5 fluid oz (¼ pint/1 gill)
190 ml	6 fluid oz
250 ml	8 fluid oz
300 ml	10 fluid oz (½ pint)
500 ml	16 fluid oz
600 ml	20 fluid oz (1 pint)
1000 ml	1¾ pints

CUPS & SPOON MEASURES

METRIC	IMPERIAL
1 ml	¼ tsp
2 ml	½ tsp
5 ml	1 tsp
15 ml	1 tbsp
60 ml	¼ cup
125 ml	½ cup
250 ml	1 cup

HELPFUL MEASURES

METRIC	IMPERIAL
3 mm	1/8 in
6 mm	¼ in
1 cm	½ in
2 cm	¾ in
2.5 cm	1 in
5 cm	2 in
6 cm	2½ in
8 cm	3 in
10 cm	4 in
13 cm	5 in
15 cm	6 in
18 cm	7 in
20 cm	8 in
23 cm	9 in
25 cm	10 in
28 cm	11 in
30 cm	12 in (1 ft)

HOW TO MEASURE

When using the graduated metric measuring cups, it is important to shake the dry ingredients loosely into the required cup. Do not tap the cup on the table, or pack the ingredients into the cup unless otherwise directed. Level top of cup with a knife. When using graduated metric measuring spoons, level top of spoon with a knife. When measuring liquids in the jug, place jug on a flat surface, check for accuracy at eye level.

OVEN TEMPERATURE

These oven temperatures are only a guide. Always check the manufacturer's manual.

	°C (Celsius)	°F (Fahrenheit)	Gas Mark
Very low	120	250	1
Low	150	300	2
Moderately low	160	325	3
Moderate	180	350	4
Moderately high	190	375	5
High	200	400	6
Very high	230	450	7

Nita Mehta's NEW RELEASES

Nita Mehta's NEW RELEASES

  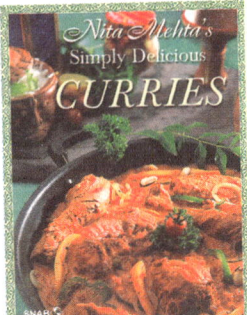 

INDIAN BOOK SHELF
55, Warren St., London W1T 5NW
Ph. : (020) 7380 0622
E-mail : indbooks@aol.com